Breaches and Bridges

German Foreign Policy in Turbulent Times

GIGA Distinguished Speaker Lecture Series

Breaches and Bridges
German Foreign Policy in Turbulent Times

Frank-Walter Steinmeier
Federal Minister for Foreign Affairs

G I G A
German Institute of Global and Area Studies
Leibniz-Institut für Globale und Regionale Studien

World Scientific

Published by

World Scientific Publishing Europe Ltd.

57 Shelton Street, Covent Garden, London WC2H 9HE

Head office: 5 Toh Tuck Link, Singapore 596224

USA office: 27 Warren Street, Suite 401-402, Hackensack, NJ 07601

Library of Congress Cataloging-in-Publication Data
Names: Steinmeier, Frank-Walter, 1956–   author.
Title: Breaches and Bridges : German foreign policy in turbulent times / Frank-Walter Steinmeier.
Description: New Jersey : World Scientific, 2017.
Identifiers: LCCN 2017007245| ISBN 9781786343659
Subjects: LCSH: Germany--Foreign relations--1990- | Hamburg
    (Germany)--Relations. | Germany--Foreign relations--Philosophy. |
    International relations--History. | International relations--Philosophy. |
    Political leadership. | International cooperation.
Classification: LCC DD290.3 .S75 2017 | DDC 327.43--dc23
LC record available at https://lccn.loc.gov/2017007245

British Library Cataloguing-in-Publication Data
A catalogue record for this book is available from the British Library.

Desk Editor at the GIGA: Julia Kramer
Desk Editors: Dong Lixi and Judy Yeo Jade Li

GIGA

German Institute of Global and Area Studies
Leibniz-Institut für Globale und Regionale Studien

Institut für Afrika-Studien
Institut für Asien-Studien
Institut für Lateinamerika-Studien

GIGA Entrance at
Neuer Jungfernstieg 21

The GIGA at the Alster

Contents

View from GIGA Headquaters on the Alster and Hamburg City Centre

Inhalt

Hamburg City Hall

Hamburg Rathausmarkt

GIGA Distinguished Speaker Lecture at the Grand Hall

Foreign Minister Steinmeier, Professor Narlikar, and First Mayor Scholz

First Mayor Scholz, Foreign Minister Steinmeier, Senator Stapelfeldt

The Esteemed Audience

Foreign Minister Steinmeier in High Demand

First Mayor Olaf Scholz

Professor Amrita Narlikar, President of the GIGA

Foreign Minister Dr Frank-Walter Steinmeier

Professor Henner Fürtig Taking Questions from the Audience

First Mayor Olaf Scholz

Welcoming Remarks

First Mayor of the Free and Hanseatic City of Hamburg
Olaf Scholz

Dear Minister,

Dear President of the Hamburg Parliament,

Dear President Professor Narlikar (GIGA),

Dear Doyenne,

Dear Representatives of the Consular Corps,

Dear Ladies and Gentlemen,

I'd like to warmly welcome you all to Hamburg Town Hall. I'm pleased with the high level of interest there is in the GIGA's work and the subjects it tackles, and the level of interest in our guest speaker, which is not surprising, of course. I would like to extend a special welcome to Foreign Minister Frank-Walter Steinmeier!

I would also like to take this opportunity to thank Professor Narlikar. The "Distinguished Speaker Lecture Series" has provided Hamburg with events that attract scholars, politicians, and the broader public in equal measure. And it all comes down to this triad: obtaining knowledge, developing options for action, and engaging in public discourse must be interconnected in a democratic, knowledge-based society. It is wonderful that we in Hamburg now have a very successful forum dedicated to these goals.

The pleasure we take in the prescient repositioning of the institute is not, however, completely unclouded: indeed, it is the crises, wars, and states of emergency in many regions of the world that make the GIGA's work so indispensable. The great number of refugees that arrived in Europe last fall and the enduring tragedies in the Mediterranean Sea have contributed to raising awareness among the broader public about issues of interdependence. For the people of Hamburg, it is palpable: what is happening in the world has consequences not only for the city, but also for particular quarters of the city and even for my own immediate neighbourhood.

Terrorism is also posing a completely new set of questions.

In these months, Europe is discovering how vulnerable it is. Vulnerable but not helpless, I would like to add.

With the EU referendum in the United Kingdom, the European Union is facing a new challenge. Despite the great disappointment at the outcome, the ties binding Europe and Great Britain have not been cut. However, they do need to be fastened differently now.

Presumably, the situation is this: a majority of British people have voted against globalisation and hope that with this vote against European integration, they can take back their own state's power to act and have increased control over the course of events. This is certainly an illusion. Only through a Union capable of action can we effectively exercise influence in the world and use globalisation to do something good for our lives. However, the fact that citizens often view the EU as a representative of this tendency towards globalisation rather than an element shaping it via democratic politics must be recognised as a problem. And in this respect, we need progress, not just in the fight against tax havens.

The same is true for the future of the Union as for the surmounting of global challenges: there is no portfolio that we can simply reach for. We have to feel our way, little by little, towards effective models and strategies. More democracy internally, more capacity for action externally – these two tasks are linked and need to be tackled simultaneously. The Union needs a joint foreign and security policy soon, not at the end of an integration process whose course cannot be precisely predicted.

The GIGA's work is extremely valuable at this particular point in time because it does not focus on current events and regions of acute crisis, as politics often does out of necessity. From their base on Neuer Jungfernstieg, the researchers look at very diverse areas in Africa, Asia, Latin America, and the Middle East – even before these generate discussion under abbreviations such as BRICS. Its scholars investigate central questions of our time, independent of whether they are currently garnering attention in the media or the political sphere. The development of terrorist rule, the increasing strength of authoritarian groupings, the long-term effects of climate change, the desired and undesired consequences of free-trade agreements – all of this and much more can be observed, and at least in part, be understood through concrete examples in the regions.

Nowhere in Europe has comparative area studies established itself as successfully as in Hamburg. The empirical findings made available by the scholarship here are important preconditions for unravelling the initially unwieldy tangle of causes and effects, and for developing preventive strategies. For this reason, I also thank the Federal Foreign Office for being on board as a reliable partner. And of course, all the employees of the GIGA.

Ladies and Gentlemen,

The global challenges call for us to utilise all the political possibilities available. The OSCE Ministerial Council, the G20, and the NATO-Russia Council are proven venues which we should maintain and further develop. This is why Hamburg, as an international trade, technology, and scholarship hub, is pleased to host the OSCE Forum in December and the economic summit of the G20 states in 2017.

Whether bilaterally or multilaterally, we want to maintain discussion – even with Russia. And of course equally so with

Turkey, which should not be allowed to distance itself further from Europe.

"The time is out of joint," says Hamlet in Shakespeare's play of the same name. This quote has been used often in recent months to emphasise the alarm over the numerous crises and wars. Yet, we should resist the temptation to give in to this alarm. We are not Hamlet. This is why we would not come up with the idea of tackling big jobs alone.

For Hamlet, the world had lost all meaning. He felt completely isolated in it. For us, it is different. We are certain that it is worthwhile to fight for a peaceful and just future. And we are aware that we can – despite the limitations of our options – achieve a great deal, as long as we stand together as democrats and allow ourselves to be guided by knowledge.

But for now, I will hand the floor over to Professor Narlikar, and after her, the Foreign Minister will talk about breaches and bridges in Germany's foreign policy. We are looking forward to it.

Thank you very much.

Grußwort

des Ersten Bürgermeisters von Hamburg
Olaf Scholz

Sehr geehrter Herr Minister,

sehr geehrte Frau Präsidentin der Hamburgischen Bürgerschaft,

sehr geehrte Frau Präsidentin Professorin Narlikar (GIGA),

sehr geehrte Frau Doyenne,

sehr geehrte Vertreterinnen und Vertreter des Konsularkorps,

meine sehr geehrten Damen und Herren,

ich begrüße Sie sehr herzlich im Hamburger Rathaus und freue mich, dass das Interesse an der Arbeit und den Themen des GIGA so groß ist – und an unserem Gastredner, was uns natürlich wenig überrascht: ein besonderes Willkommen an den Außenminister Frank-Walter Steinmeier!

Auch meinen Dank an Frau Narlikar möchte ich gleich vorneweg schicken: Mit den „Distinguished Speaker Lectures" hat Hamburg eine Veranstaltungsreihe bekommen, welche

Wissenschaftler, Politiker und eine breitere Öffentlichkeit gleichermaßen anzieht. Und auf diesen Dreiklang kommt es an: Das Gewinnen von Erkenntnissen, das Entwickeln von Handlungsoptionen und der Diskurs der Öffentlichkeit müssen in der demokratischen Wissensgesellschaft verbunden sein. Dass wir in Hamburg nun ein sehr erfolgreiches Forum bekommen haben, welches genau dies leistet, ist großartig.

Die Freude darüber, wie vorausschauend die Neupositionierung dieses Instituts war, kann allerdings nicht ganz ungetrübt sein: Denn es sind unter anderem die Krisen, Kriege und Notlagen in vielen Regionen der Welt, welche die Arbeit des GIGA so notwendig machen. Dabei haben die vielen Flüchtlinge, die im vergangenen Herbst in Europa ankamen, und die andauernden Tragödien auf dem Mittelmeer das Bewusstsein für die Interdependenz in der breiten Öffentlichkeit wachsen lassen. Auch die Hamburgerinnen und Hamburger spüren deutlich: Was in der Welt vor sich geht, hat nicht nur Folgen für die Stadt, sondern sogar für den Stadtteil und meine eigene, direkte Nachbarschaft.

Auch der Terror wirft völlig neue Fragen auf.

Europa muss in diesen Monaten erfahren, wie verletzlich es ist. Verletzlich, aber nicht hilflos, möchte ich hinzufügen.

Mit dem Ausgang des Referendums im Vereinigten Königreich ist eine neue Herausforderung auf die Union zugekommen. Bei aller Enttäuschung über den Ausgang des EU-Referendums: Die Bande zwischen Europa und Großbritannien sind nicht abgerissen, sie müssen jetzt aber auf eine andere Weise geknüpft werden.

Vermutlich ist es so: Eine Mehrheit der Briten hat gegen die Globalisierung gestimmt und hofft, mit diesem Votum gegen die europäische Integration Handlungsmöglichkeiten des eigenen Staates und mehr Einfluss auf den Gang der Dinge zurückgewinnen zu können. Das ist sicher eine Illusion. Nur durch eine handlungsfähige Union können wir wirksam Einfluss in der Welt nehmen und aus der Globalisierung etwas Gutes für unser Leben machen. Dass die EU den Bürgerinnen und Bürgern oft als Repräsentantin eben dieser Globalisierungstendenz gilt und nicht als Element ihrer Gestaltung mittels demokratischer Politik, muss allerdings als Problem erkannt werden. Und in dieser Hinsicht brauchen wir Fortschritte; nicht nur beim Kampf gegen Steueroasen.

Für die Zukunft der Union gilt dabei das Gleiche wie für die Bewältigung der globalen Herausforderungen: Es gibt kein Portfolio, auf das wir einfach zurückgreifen könnten. An wirksame Modelle und Strategien müssen wir uns erst peu à peu herantasten. Mehr Demokratie nach innen, mehr Handlungsfähigkeit nach außen – diese beiden Aufgaben hängen zusammen und müssen parallel angepackt werden. Die Union braucht eine gemeinsame Außen- und Sicherheitspolitik schon bald und nicht erst am Ende eines Integrationsprozesses, dessen Verlauf sich nicht exakt vorhersagen lässt.

Die Arbeit des GIGA ist gerade jetzt ausgesprochen wertvoll, denn sie konzentriert sich nicht auf aktuelle Ereignisse und akute Krisenregionen, wie es die Politik notwendigerweise häufig tun muss. Die Forscherinnen und Forscher nehmen vom Neuen Jungfernstieg aus ganz unterschiedliche Gebiete in Afrika, Asien, Lateinamerika und Nahost in den Blick, bevor diese unter Kürzeln wie BRICS von sich reden machen. Sie untersuchen zentrale Fragestellungen unserer Zeit, unabhängig davon, ob diese in den Medien oder der Politik gerade Gehör finden. Das Entstehen terroristischer Herrschaft, das Erstarken autoritärer Gruppierungen, die langfristigen Auswirkungen des Klimawandels, die erwünschten und unerwünschten Folgen von Freihandelsabkommen – all das und vieles mehr lässt sich in den Regionen an konkreten Beispielen beobachten und zumindest in Teilen verstehen.

Nirgendwo in Europa hat sich die vergleichende Regionalforschung so erfolgreich etabliert wie in Hamburg. Die empirischen Erkenntnisse, welche die Wissenschaft hier zur Verfügung stellt, sind eine wichtige Voraussetzung, um das zunächst unüberschaubar scheinende Geflecht aus Ursachen und Wirkungen zu entwirren und präventive Strategien zu entwickeln. Deshalb an dieser Stelle noch einmal meinen Dank an das Auswärtige Amt, dass es als verlässlicher Partner mit an Bord ist. Und natürlich an alle Mitarbeiterinnen und Mitarbeiter des GIGA.

Meine Damen und Herren,

die globalen Herausforderungen rufen danach, dass wir alle politischen Möglichkeiten nutzen. OSZE-Ministerrat, G20 und NATO-Russland-Rat sind bewährte Formate, die wir pflegen und weiterentwickeln sollten. Deshalb ist Hamburg als internationaler Handels-, Technik- und Wissenschaftsstandort gerne Gastgeberin für das OSZE-Forum im Dezember und für den Wirtschaftsgipfel der G20-Staaten 2017.

Ob bi- oder multilateral – wir wollen im Gespräch bleiben, auch mit Russland. Und natürlich ebenso mit der Türkei, die sich nicht weiter von Europa entfernen darf.

Die Zeit, sagt Hamlet in Shakespeares Stück, das seinen Namen trägt, die Zeit sei aus den Fugen – „The time is out of joint". Das Zitat wurde in den vergangenen Monaten besonders häufig bemüht, wenn es darum ging, dem Erschrecken über die zahlreichen Krisen und Kriege Ausdruck zu verleihen. Doch wir sollten der Versuchung widerstehen, uns diesem Erschrecken hinzugeben –, wir sind nicht Hamlet. Deshalb kämen wir auch nicht auf die Idee, große Aufgaben alleine anzugehen.

Für Hamlet hat die Welt jeden Sinn verloren, er fühlt sich in ihr nur noch fremd. Das ergeht uns ganz anders. Wir sind uns sicher, dass es sich lohnt, für eine friedliche und gerechte Zukunft zu kämpfen. Und wir sind uns bewusst, dass wir – bei allem Wissen um die Beschränktheit unserer Möglichkeiten – vieles erreichen können, solange wir als Demokraten zusammenstehen und uns von Erkenntnis leiten lassen.

Aber nun übergebe ich das Wort an Frau Professorin Narlikar, und danach wird der Außenminister über Brüche und Brücken deutscher Außenpolitik sprechen. Wir sind gespannt.

Vielen Dank.

Professor Amrita Narlikar, President of the GIGA

Setting the Stage

President of the
GIGA German Institute of Global and Area Studies
Leibniz-Institut für Globale und Regionale Studien
Amrita Narlikar

Introduction

The world today is caught up in a series of conflicts and crises. A random selection of these challenges is illustrative of their wide geographical range, cross-regional spillovers, and possible contagion effects: for example, the war in Syria, the dispute over Crimea, the multiple crises hitting Europe, and the severe threat to the global multilateral trading system resulting from rising US disengagement and heightened protectionism. Equally striking is the very limited success that international organisations have had, thus far, in managing these proliferating crises; some, in fact, have not only failed to manage the problems, but have found their own existence imperilled by these failures. There is no dearth of opinions on the problems that the world faces, as is clear from the vibrant use of social media for political expression. But the peculiar pathologies of social media often only reinforce the engulfing darkness that W.B. Yeats had identified in *The Second Coming*: "The best lack all conviction, while the worst are full of passionate intensity." Surrounded by this growing cacaphony and rising disorder, it is all too easy to despair.

The "Distinguished Speaker Lecture Series", conceptualised and organised by the GIGA German Institute of Global and Area Studies, aims to offer a small pathway out of the despair and towards an element of hope. It brings together some of the best and the brightest minds to address the key problems of our times. Distinguished speakers at GIGA include some of the top scholars who have served as pioneers in their disciplines. But the lecture series is envisaged as one that includes practitioners who have influenced the world of policy. This is because, at the GIGA, we firmly believe that academia has much to gain from interaction with the world of practice, and vice versa. Practitioners can help researchers by injecting our theories with a healthy dose of reality, and also encouraging them to take into account the feasibility of any solutions we propose to real-world problems. Scholars, in turn, can assist practitioners with their empirical knowledge and creative ideas, and also help in developing longer-term solutions (and not only fight the fires that policy-makers often have to immediately attend to). This two-way interaction seems to be especially important today, given the range and scale of problems that the world is saddled with. In its commitment to policy engagement at all stages of its research – from conceptualisation to dissemination – the GIGA also stands true to the Leibniz motto of *Theoria cum Praxi*. This is why, the Institute was especially happy and honoured when Germany's Federal Foreign Minister, Frank-Walter Steinmeier, agreed to deliver the inaugural lecture of the practitioners' part of its "Distinguished Speaker Lecture Series".

Our honourable speaker, Minister Steinmeier, has had a long and illustrious career in government. When he delivered this lecture, he had been serving as Germany's Federal Minister for Foreign Affairs since 2013 – a role that he fulfilled until February 2017, after which, he took up the position of the Federal President of Germany. Since 1998, he has served on four cabinets, and also as the leader of the parliamentary opposition. His previous positions have included serving as Head of the State Chancellery, his first term as Foreign Minister, Deputy Chancellor, and Chair of the SPD Parliamentary Group. His academic training is in Law and Political Science. His high credentials, moreover, are illustrated not only by his academic training and the positions he has held, but the innovative ideas and experience that he brings to the field. His achievements are too numerous to list in this introduction, but further details can be found at the end of this book. At this point, suffice it to note that for all those interested in the study of negotiation and diplomacy, Minister Steinmeier's negotiation skills across different issue-areas and his ability to break deadlocks have won him many admirers. Under his leadership as Foreign Minister, Germany has come to play an increasingly important role as a responsible international stakeholder. This role and leadership are especially important in the difficult times we live in. Especially at a time when liberalism is facing greater challenges across different parts of the globe, other world leaders could do a lot worse than follow his example of combining expertise and experience with integrity as well as the "conviction" that Yeats had called for.

The commitment of this Lecture Series is to bring some of the most distinguished thinkers to Hamburg, and to engage with our policy and scholarly communities as well as the interested public. We are grateful for the commitment that the city has shown us in return at all levels. Here, a special note of thanks is due to our First Mayor – Olaf Scholz – for his support of the GIGA on all matters, and also his personal presence as host at this important event. The venue is significant: we are at the Rathaus – the imposing and grand Town Hall – of Free and Hanseatic Hamburg. This beautiful setting is a powerful reminder of Hamburg's history as an open-minded and welcoming city, which prides itself as a gateway to the world. We hope that this city – with its plethora of research institutes of international excellence – will continue to serve as a source of homegrown intellectual ideas and also as a conduit for inspiring ideas from all over the world, which could facilitate Germany's and Europe's constructive and vital role in global and local affairs.

Identifying the Problems

There are several international political and economic problems that need addressing. By way of example, I outline just a few here. All these problems pose serious threats to the post-World War II liberal order, and illustrate the urgent need for smart solutions, clear-sighted leadership, and coordinated action.

Backlash Against Globalisation[1]

Globalisation – the increasing integration among countries and peoples via the movement of goods, services, capital, labour, images and ideas across borders – has served us well for the past decades in the past. The economic data is clear: trade, migration, and at least certain forms of global financial integration have generated growth and prosperity worldwide. Admittedly, not all countries have benefitted equally, and the picture is even more mixed within countries. But overall, the general trends show that globalisation is a rising tide that lifts countries and classes. The positive impact of globalisation can be even higher within countries if appropriate social contracts are in place between governments and societies. And yet, in the face of ample evidence, extreme disillusionment and dissatisfaction with globalisation has set in.

The backlash against globalisation is no longer a fringe movement. Witness the strong anti-trade sentiment expressed, for instance in the US Presidential debates as well as the result of the Brexit referendum in the UK, and it becomes very clear

---

[1]   The author presented some of these arguments in Amrita Narlikar, Globalisierung neu aushandeln. In: Wolfgang Ischinger and Dirk Messner (eds.), *Deutschlands neue Verantwortung. Die Zukunft der deutschen und europäischen Außen-, Entwicklungs- und Sicherheitspolitik*, Berlin: Econ Verlag, 2017.

that anti-globalisation has entered the mainstream. The turn to right-wing nationalism on the one hand, and radicalisation on the other, are both (in part) reactions of people to what they see as the failed promise of globalisation. Multilateral trade negotiations, organised under the rubric of the WTO's Doha Development Agenda, have been badly deadlocked. Mega-regionals, such as the Transatlantic Trade and Investment Partnership and the Transatlantic Pacific Partnership, risk meeting their end even before they have begun. Nations are threatening to put up physical and policy walls against immigrants. If anti-globalisation does indeed result in de-globalisation, the costs will be high for the system as a whole. And while everyone would be adversely affected by de-globalisation, the costs will be significantly higher for the poor than for the rich. Finding ways to secure the positive aspects of globalisation, and reduce the negative ones, needs to be a priority for scholars and practitioners today.

Institutions of Cooperation under Threat

Several international institutions, which were set up in the aftermath of World War II, are now deadlocked. The multilateral trade regime – governed by the General Agreement on Tariffs and Trade and then the WTO – is but one example. The United Nations, including the UN Security Council, and its failure to act over such major crises as Syria and Crimea is another. The successes of the Paris Conference (2015) in the climate change negotiations potentially face a new challenge with the incoming

US administration expressing some skepticism on the phenomenon of climate change. Recurrent deadlocks of this type are damaging not only for particular causes, but are also triggers for vicious cycles of declining credibility that then makes it even harder for international organisations to deliver results.

Important reason for the proliferation of deadlocks in multilateral settings is the emergence of too many key players occupying or aspiring to seats at the high table. Difficulties in reaching consensus have been further exacerbated by the fact that today's multipolarity is underpinned by polarisation and difference.[2] The multiple players at the negotiating table today do not constitute a club of like-minded countries; rather, they bring together players like the US and the EU with China, Brazil, India and Russia i.e. countries at very different stages of development, shaped by very different historical trajectories, and driven by very different value systems. It is perhaps not surprising that it has been difficult for such a motley group of countries to reach agreement on anything of consequence. But just how frayed any semblance of a consensus has now become is clear with even a cursory look at the EU.

The European Union offers quite a different model of cooperative action from multilateralism. Having learnt the hard lessons of the first half of the 20th century, visionaries from European countries recognised the merits of economic integration

---

2   Amrita Narlikar, *Deadlocks in Multilateral Negotiations: Causes and Solutions,* Cambridge: Cambridge University Press, 2010.

as an important step towards building a sustainable peace. Even in the expanded EU, the scale of difference among member countries is much smaller in comparison to the multilateral level. An elaborate set of institutions and rules had managed to maintain and facilitate deepening integration. But a series of crises has continued to hit the EU in recent years.

Greece and the eurozone crisis showed the difficulties of running a monetary union without a fiscal one, while the immigration crisis illustrated just how divided the community was not only on the political and economic costs of burden-sharing but also on the ethical questions. A largely unanticipated blow then came in the form of the referendum in the UK in June 2016, with the Brexit campaign achieving a narrow but critical win. The proclaimed commitment of a core member of the EU to exit the club is unprecedented, and risks encouraging similar tendencies from other anti-immigration, nationalistic, atavistic groups in parts of Europe. Much depends now on how the EU deals with Britain subsequent to its invoking Article 50 this year. A minimal and necessary condition for the EU to survive Brexit is a very tough message in place that makes the costs of leaving the EU clear and also acts as a deterrent to others considering the possibility. The main point at hand, however, is the fact that even a very well-established institution of relatively like-minded countries, with high levels of deep integration, now faces the risk of division over financial issues, deadlock over immigration issues, and even breakdown over Brexit. With relatively strong institutions such as the EU facing an existential crisis, it is hardly surprising that others with much larger memberships, much greater diversity, and much fewer unifying ideals (such as the UN or the WTO) are also flailing.

The Return of Geopolitics

Some might argue that it is misguided to speak of the *return* of geopolitics when geopolitical considerations had never gone away, especially as far as large parts of the developing world are concerned. However, the world that we see today is indeed very far removed from what was described in such seminal works as Francis Fukuyama's *The End of History* and Thomas Friedman's *The World is Flat.* Today, old-fashioned power political games are back with a vengeance[3] – take, for instance, the power struggle in the Middle East among regional and great powers, or the sovereignty dispute between Russia and Ukraine in Crimea, or China's adventurism and expansionism in its neighbouring seas. In some cases – such as Syria – localised border disputes rapidly escalate to having global impact via migration, radicalisation, and the spread of extremism. Combine these different threats with the aforementioned problem – deadlocked international institutions – and negotiated solutions seem ever more elusive.

---

[3] Walter Russell Mead, The Return of Geopolitics: The Revenge of the Revisionist Powers, *Foreign Affairs*, 93, May-June, 2014.

Conceptualising Solutions

The problems outlined above pose a fundamental challenge to existing theories; be they neo-liberal institutionalism that had promised prosperity and peace to the world via the logic of institution building, or constructivism that assured us of the high likelihood of socialisation via increasing cooperative interactions. What might be done in the face of these challenges? I suggest below three sets of recommendations.

Recommendation 1:
Engage with the "Others" – Because They Matter[4]

One of the reasons why globalisation is under challenge, why multilateral deadlocks are recurring, and why countries are moving away from liberal institutionalist solutions to geopolitical ones is because there has been far too little consultation with diverse stakeholders on the purpose of the various international cooperative endeavours that have underpinned the post-World War II era. A fundamental rethinking is necessary on which global public goods different stakeholders consider as high priorities, and are also willing to share the costs for.

This means engaging with developing countries that had lacked agenda-setting power when the grand bargains of 1945 were made, and also excluded groups within developed and developing countries. This engagement, moreover, must be real

---

[4] Amrita Narlikar, "Because They Matter": Recognise Diversity, Globalise Research, *GIGA Focus Global 1,* April 2016, accessed at https://www.giga-hamburg.de/en/publication/because-they-matter on 15 January 2017.

and substantive, rather than a resort to the tokenism of political correctness; giving a seat to the token representatives from poor countries in negotiating forums or academic conferences will simply not suffice. Even for those countries of the Global South that have representation at various international forums, we in the West have often viewed them through our own lenses and expected them to replicate our own behaviour patterns. In fact, what is needed is a far better understanding of the world-views, aspirations, and goals of different world regions and populations – whether they are directly represented in important groupings like the G20 or exercise indirect voice via coalitions with other developing countries.

Fundamental to this engagement is a close collaboration between researchers and practitioners. Cutting-edge research on the hopes, expectations, and challenges from regions that lie beyond the EU and the US, and also their philosophical traditions and historical trajectories, is indispensable to get this process going. This, in fact, is precisely the kind of research that we are developing at the GIGA, and why we emphasise the importance of adopting a "global approach" to scholarship. We hope that some of our research findings will help Western scholars and governments understand the Global South on its own terms. We thus believe that we may be able to serve as an intellectual bridge between the EU/ US and the great majority of countries that have come to matter far more than has yet been recognised.[5]

---

[5]   Further details of this research agenda can be found in Narlikar 2016.

Importantly, understanding does not mean conceding to the demands of one's negotiating counterparts. Rather, understanding is important because it can help one identify and communicate one's red lines. If taken on in the right spirit, this process can be crucial for reducing the scope for misperception and misunderstanding, and also potentially facilitate the creative redefinition of negotiating space within mutually recognised constraints.

Recommendation 2:
Compensate those who lose out from globalisation

While globalisation produces aggregate gains, it also generates losses for certain groups within countries. This is where domestic leadership is critical. Although social contracts vary greatly with national political cultures, governments must find ways to share the gains from liberalisation within their populations. National economic cultures differ and depend very much on particular norms. Hence, programmes to better distribute the gains and losses must be home-grown.

It is important here to note that international organisations can help in finding some collective solutions via research, via advice, and via aid and trade policies. But ultimately, institutions of global governance have only limited control over what member countries do to better distribute the gains from globalisation. An important role that national leaders can and should play is therefore to avoid the temptation to scapegoat international trade agreements and close borders to qualified migrants. Such moves can considerably worsen the existing problem by triggering retaliation from other economies, and also generate a heavy cost for the poorest consumers in the country that implements protectionist policies.

International organisations may have a bigger role to play, especially if the world continues to go in the direction of fragmentation. They could, for instance, complement the social contracts of member countries with international social contracts that offer more equitable terms of voice, exchange, and burden-sharing. To do this effectively, international negotiators would be well served to engage more seriously with their diverse negotiating counterparts on the question of global public goods, as outlined under Recommendation 1.

Recommendation 3:
Sell the successes of globalisation more effectively

For most scholars and practitioners, the gains from globalisation are so clear that the case does not need repeating. But the costs of this complacency have been very high, especially when posited against the ill-informed but passionate intensity of the anti-globalisers. They were most clearly borne out in the case of the Brexit referendum, where the "Remain" campaign did little to explain the benefits of EU membership to the population. If globalisation is to survive, the intellectual case has to be reiterated, and it must also be effectively translated in the popular domain.

Such an initiative would again need strong cooperation between academics and practitioners, and would require the deepening of existing outreach processes and the creation of new ones. Without popular support, even a reformed, updated, and equitable bargain over globalisation is unlikely to survive.

Conclusion

To help us grapple with some of these issues, and to show us pathways whereby innovative and feasible solutions might be implemented, we have with us a thinker and doer who has always led by example – Minister Frank-Walter Steinmeier. We are greatly looking forward to his analysis.

Den Weg bereiten

Präsidentin des
GIGA German Institute of Global and Area Studies
Leibniz-Institut für Globale und Regionale Studien
Amrita Narlikar

Einführung

Die Welt wird derzeit von zahlreichen Konflikten und Krisen geschüttelt. Schon eine willkürliche Auswahl dieser Herausforderungen illustriert ihre große geografische Reichweite, ihre überregionalen Auswirkungen und mögliche Ansteckungsgefahr: Da wären der Krieg in Syrien, die Auseinandersetzung über die Krim, die zahlreichen Krisen Europas und die gravierende Bedrohung des multilateralen Welthandelssystems durch die zunehmende Abschottung der USA und den wachsenden Protektionismus. Ebenso frappierend ist der bisher sehr begrenzte Erfolg internationaler Organisationen bei der Bekämpfung dieser ausufernden Krisen; einige dieser Organisationen sind tatsächlich nicht nur an der Problembewältigung gescheitert, sondern sehen sich durch dieses

Scheitern sogar in ihrer eignen Existenz bedroht. Wie an der lebhaften Nutzung sozialer Medien für politische Äußerungen leicht erkennbar ist, herrscht kein Mangel an Meinungen zu den Problemen der Welt. Doch die eigentümlichen Pathologien der sozialen Medien verstärken oft nur die allumfassende Düsternis, die W. B. Yeats in seinem Gedicht *The Second Coming* (*Das zweite Kommen*) wahrnahm: „Den Besten fehlt jegliche Überzeugung, während die Schlechtesten voll leidenschaftlicher Intensität sind."[1] Angesichts dieser immer lauter werdenden Kakofonie und des zunehmenden Chaos kann man leicht verzweifeln.

Die vom GIGA German Institute of Global and Area Studies/ Leibniz-Institut für Globale und Regionale Studien konzipierte und organisierte „Distinguished Speaker Lecture Series" soll einen kleinen Ausweg aus der Verzweiflung bieten und ein wenig Hoffnung machen. Hier versammeln sich einige der besten und hellsten Köpfe, um die wichtigsten Probleme unserer Zeit anzugehen. Unter den hoch geschätzten Gästen sind einige Geistesgrößen, die in ihrer jeweiligen akademischen Disziplin Pionierarbeit leisten. In der Vortragsreihe sollen außerdem Persönlichkeiten aus der Praxis zu Wort kommen, die die Welt der Politik mitprägen, denn am GIGA sind wir fest davon überzeugt, dass die Wissenschaft aus der Interaktion mit der Praxis großen Nutzen ziehen kann – und umgekehrt. Praktikerinnen und Praktiker können uns in der Wissenschaft helfen, unseren Theorien eine gesunde Dosis Realität zu geben. Und wenn wir Lösungen für die Probleme der Welt vorschlagen, können sie uns darin bestärken,

---

[1] Eigene Übersetzung.

deren Machbarkeit im Blick zu behalten. Wissenschaftlerinnen und Wissenschaftler wiederum können denen, die in der Praxis arbeiten, mit ihrem empirischen Wissen und ihren kreativen Ideen zur Seite stehen und auch bei der Entwicklung längerfristiger Lösungen assistieren (und nicht nur bei der Bekämpfung der Brandherde, um die sich die Politik oft unmittelbar kümmern muss). Angesichts der Bandbreite und des Ausmaßes der die Welt belastende Probleme scheint diese wechselseitige Interaktion heute besonders wichtig. Im Bemühen um politisches Engagement in allen Phasen der Forschung – vom Konzeptentwurf bis zur Veröffentlichung – macht sich das GIGA auch das Motto der Leibniz-Gemeinschaft *Theoria cum Praxi* zu eigen. Deshalb fühlte sich das Institut besonders geehrt und glücklich, als der deutsche Außenminister Frank-Walter Steinmeier zusagte, den Eröffnungsvortrag des praxisorientierten Teils der „Distinguished Speaker Lecture Series" zu halten.

Unser geschätzter Vortragsredner, Minister Steinmeier, blickt auf eine lange und glänzende Regierungslaufbahn zurück. Als er seinen Vortrag hielt, war er seit 2013 deutscher Außenminister. Dieses Amt füllte er bis Februar 2017 aus, als er zum deutschen Bundespräsidenten gewählt wurde. Seit 1998 gehörte er vier Kabinetten an und war außerdem Oppositionsführer im Bundestag. Zu seinen früheren Positionen gehören unter anderem Chef des Bundeskanzleramtes, eine erste Amtszeit als Außenminister, Vizekanzler und Fraktionsvorsitzender der SPD. Er hat Rechtswissenschaften und Politikwissenschaften studiert. Seine außerordentliche Qualifikation wird überdies nicht nur in seiner akademischen Ausbildung und seinen beruflichen Stationen sichtbar, sondern auch in den innovativen Ideen und der Erfahrung, die er mit einbringt. Seine Erfolge sind zu zahlreich, um sie in dieser Einführung aufzulisten, weitere Einzelheiten finden sich jedoch am Ende dieses Buches. An dieser Stelle soll der Hinweis genügen, dass Minister Steinmeiers Verhandlungsgeschick in verschiedenen Gemengelagen und seine Fähigkeit, festgefahrene Situationen aufzubrechen, ihm unter all denen, die sich für Verhandlungsführung und Diplomatie interessieren, zahlreiche Bewunderer beschert haben. Unter seiner Führung als Außenminister übernahm Deutschland eine zunehmend wichtigere Rolle als verantwortungsvoller Akteur auf dem internationalen Parkett. In unseren schwierigen Zeiten sind diese Rolle und Führungsqualität von besonderer Bedeutung. Vor allem in einer Zeit, in der der Liberalismus in verschiedenen Teilen der Welt immer stärker in Bedrängnis gerät, könnten andere führende Politikerinnen und Politiker schlechter beraten sein, als seinem Beispiel zu folgen und Sachverstand und Erfahrung mit Integrität und der von Yeats vermissten „Überzeugung" zu verbinden.

Das erklärte Ziel dieser Vortragsreihe ist es, einige der profiliertesten Geistesgrößen nach Hamburg zu holen und mit der politischen und wissenschaftlichen Gemeinschaft sowie mit der interessierten Öffentlichkeit ins Gespräch zu bringen. Wir sind dankbar für den Rückhalt, mit dem uns die Stadt im Gegenzug in jeder Hinsicht begegnet. Hier gilt ein besonderer Dank unserem Ersten Bürgermeister – Olaf Scholz – für seine umfassende Unterstützung des GIGA und seine persönliche Anwesenheit als Gastgeber bei dieser wichtigen Begegnung. Der Ort ist bedeutungsvoll: Wir befinden uns im prachtvollen und imposanten großen Saal des Rathauses der Freien und Hansestadt Hamburg. Diese schöne Kulisse erinnert eindrucksvoll an die Geschichte Hamburgs als einer aufgeschlossenen und einladenden Stadt, die sich stolz als Tor zur Welt präsentiert. Wir hoffen, dass diese Stadt – mit ihrer Vielzahl an international herausragenden Forschungseinrichtungen – weiterhin ein Nährboden für das heimische Geistesleben und ein Anziehungspunkt für inspirierende Ideen aus der ganzen Welt sein wird, die die konstruktive und wichtige Rolle Deutschlands und Europas in globalen und lokalen Angelegenheiten begünstigen werden.

Die Probleme benennen

Es gibt etliche internationale politische und wirtschaftliche Probleme, die es anzugehen gilt. Ich werde hier nur einige davon exemplarisch umreißen. All diese Probleme stellen ernste Gefahren für die liberale Ordnung dar, die nach dem Zweiten Weltkrieg etabliert wurde, und illustrieren den dringenden Bedarf an intelligenten Lösungen, vorausschauender Führungskompetenz und koordiniertem Handeln.

Auflehnung gegen die Globalisierung[2]

Die Globalisierung – die zunehmende Integration von Ländern

---

[2] Die Autorin hat einige dieser Argumente dargestellt in: Amrita Narlikar, Globalisierung neu aushandeln. In: Wolfgang Ischinger und Dirk Messner (Hrsg.), *Deutschlands neue Verantwortung. Die Zukunft der deutschen und europäischen Außen-, Entwicklungs- und Sicherheitspolitik*, Berlin: Econ Verlag, 2017.

und Bevölkerungen durch den grenzüberschreitenden Austausch von Gütern, Dienstleistungen, Kapital, Arbeit, Vorstellungen und Ideen – bewährt sich seit vielen Jahrzehnten. Die ökonomischen Daten sind eindeutig: Handel, Migration und zumindest bestimmte Formen der globalen Finanzintegration haben weltweit Wachstum und Wohlstand hervorgebracht. Zugegeben: Nicht alle Länder haben gleichermaßen profitiert und innerhalb der Länder ist das Bild noch uneinheitlicher. Doch im Großen und Ganzen zeigen die allgemeinen Entwicklungen, dass die Globalisierung eine steigende Flut ist, die Länder und gesellschaftliche Schichten empor hebt. Mit geeigneten Gesellschaftsverträgen zwischen Regierung und Gesellschaft kann sich die Globalisierung innerhalb der Länder sogar noch positiver auswirken. Dennoch hat eine extreme Desillusionierung und Unzufriedenheit mit der Globalisierung eingesetzt.

Die Gegenbewegung zur Globalisierung ist keine Randerscheinung mehr. Betrachten wir beispielsweise die vehemente Ablehnung des Freihandels, wie sie in den Präsidentschaftsdebatten der USA zum Ausdruck kam, ebenso wie das Ergebnis des Brexit-Referendums im Vereinigten Königreich, dann müssen wir feststellen, dass die Globalisierungsfeindlichkeit im Mainstream angekommen ist. Die Hinwendung zum Rechtsnationalismus auf der einen und die Radikalisierung auf der anderen Seite sind (zum Teil) Reaktionen der Menschen auf das ihrem Eindruck nach gebrochene Versprechen der Globalisierung. Die multilateralen Handelsgespräche im Kontext der WTO-Entwicklungsagenda von Doha sind vollkommen festgefahren.

Mega-regionale Freihandelsabkommen wie etwa die Transatlantic Trade and Investment Partnership und die Transatlantic Pacific Partnership sind unter Umständen am Ende, noch bevor sie überhaupt begonnen haben. Nationen drohen, physische und politische Mauern gegen Migration zu errichten. Sollte die Antiglobalisierung tatsächlich in eine Deglobalisierung münden, dann wird das System als Ganzes einen sehr hohen Preis dafür bezahlen müssen. Wobei die Deglobalisierung zwar allen schaden, den Armen aber erheblich mehr abverlangen würde als den Reichen. Die Suche nach Mitteln und Wegen, um die positiven Aspekte der Globalisierung zu sichern und die negativen zu mindern, muss heute allen Fachkräften aus Wissenschaft und Praxis ein vorrangiges Anliegen sein.

Institutionen der Zusammenarbeit gefährdet

Mehrere internationale Institutionen, die nach dem Zweiten Weltkrieg geschaffen wurden, stecken heute in der Sackgasse. Das multilaterale Handelssystem – zunächst durch das Allgemeine Zoll- und Handelsabkommen GATT und dann durch die WTO geregelt – ist nur ein Beispiel dafür. Ein weiteres sind die Vereinten Nationen, einschließlich des UNO-Sicherheitsrats, und ihre Handlungsunfähigkeit in so gewaltigen Krisen wie in Syrien und um die Krim. Die Verhandlungserfolge der Pariser Klimakonferenz (2015) in puncto Bekämpfung des Klimawandels sehen sich durch die neue US-Regierung, die sich als Klimaskeptiker gibt, möglicherweise schon neuen

Herausforderungen gegenüber. Wiederholte Rückschläge dieser Art schaden nicht nur den konkreten Anliegen, sondern können außerdem einen Teufelskreis einleiten, in dem die Glaubwürdigkeit internationaler Organisationen schwindet und es ihnen so weiter erschwert wird, Ergebnisse zu erzielen.

Ein wichtiger Grund für die sich mehrenden Blockaden in multilateralen Kontexten ist das Auftreten zu vieler wichtiger Player, die mit am Verhandlungstisch sitzen oder sitzen wollen. Dass die heutige Multipolarität auf Polarisierung und Gegensätzen basiert, macht die Konsensbildung noch schwieriger.[3] Heute bilden die zahlreichen Player am Verhandlungstisch keinen Klub gleichgesinnter Länder; vielmehr treffen hier Akteure wie die USA und die EU mit China, Brasilien, Indien und Russland zusammen, d. h. Länder in sehr unterschiedlichen Entwicklungsstadien, die von sehr unterschiedlichen Geschichtsverläufen geprägt sind und sich von ganz verschiedenen Wertesystemen leiten lassen. Es ist vielleicht nicht überraschend, dass es für eine so heterogene Länderrunde bislang schwierig ist, sich auf irgendetwas von Belang zu einigen. Doch wie sehr schon der bloße Anschein von Konsensfähigkeit inzwischen zerfasert ist, wird bereits bei einem flüchtigen Blick auf die EU klar.

Die Europäische Union offeriert ein ganz anderes Kooperationsmodell als der Multilateralismus. Nach den bitteren Lektionen aus der ersten Hälfte des 20. Jahrhunderts erkannten Visionäre aus europäischen Ländern in den Vorzügen der wirtschaftlichen Integration einen

---

[3] Amrita Narlikar, *Deadlocks in Multilateral Negotiations: Causes and Solutions*, Cambridge: Cambridge University Press, 2010.

wichtigen Schritt zum Aufbau eines nachhaltigen Friedens. Selbst in der erweiterten EU sind die Unterschiede zwischen den Mitgliedstaaten im Vergleich zur multilateralen Ebene viel geringer. Mit einem ausgeklügelten System von Institutionen und Regeln gelang es, den Integrationsprozess und seine Vertiefung zu verstetigen und zu begünstigen. Doch seit einigen Jahren wird die EU fortwährend von Krisen erschüttert.

Griechenland und die Krise des Euro-Raums haben gezeigt, wie schwierig es ist, eine Währungsunion ohne Fiskalunion zu steuern, während die Migrationskrise deutlich machte, wie weit die Auffassungen innerhalb der Gemeinschaft nicht nur über die politischen und wirtschaftlichen Kosten einer Lastenteilung, sondern auch über die ethischen Fragen auseinander liegen. Ein weitgehend unerwarteter Schlag kam dann im Juni 2016 in Form des Referendums im Vereinigten Königreich, bei dem die Brexit-Kampagne einen knappen, aber entscheidenden Sieg errang. Die erklärte Absicht eines Kernmitglieds der EU, den Klub zu verlassen, ist ohne Beispiel und könnte ähnliche Tendenzen bei anderen Einwanderungsgegnern, nationalistischen, atavistischen Gruppen in Teilen Europas bestärken. Es hängt viel davon ab, wie die EU mit Großbritannien umgeht, nachdem in diesem Jahr Artikel 50 Anwendung fand. Eine notwendige Mindestvoraussetzung, damit die EU den Brexit übersteht, ist eine unmissverständliche Aussage, die den Preis für den Austritt aus der EU deutlich vor Augen führt und auf andere, die diese Möglichkeit in Erwägung ziehen, abschreckend wirkt. Der wichtigste Punkt jedoch ist die Tatsache, dass selbst eine gut etablierte Institution relativ gleichgesinnter Länder mit ausgesprochen tief greifendem Integrationsgrad nun Gefahr läuft, sich wegen Finanzanliegen zu spalten, sich wegen Einwanderungsfragen zu blockieren und wegen des Brexits gar zusammenzubrechen. Wenn schon die EU mit ihren relativ starken Institutionen in einer existenziellen Krise steckt, dann verwundert es kaum, dass andere Organisationen mit viel mehr Mitgliedern, viel größerer Vielfalt und viel weniger einenden Wertvorstellungen (wie zum Beispiel die Vereinten Nationen oder die WTO) ebenfalls ins Trudeln geraten.

Die Rückkehr der Geopolitik

Manche mögen einwenden, es sei nicht passend, von einer *Rückkehr* der Geopolitik zu sprechen, da geopolitische Überlegungen niemals ganz von der Bildfläche verschwunden waren, insbesondere nicht im Hinblick auf weite Teile des globalen Südens. Dennoch hat sich die Welt, wie sie sich uns heute darstellt, tatsächlich deutlich von dem entfernt, was in so bahnbrechenden Werken wie Francis Fukuyamas *Das Ende der Geschichte* und Thomas Friedmans *Die Welt ist flach* beschrieben wird. Heute haben wir es wieder vehement mit antiquierten politischen Machtspielen zu tun[4] – so zum Beispiel dem Machtkampf zwischen Regional- und Großmächten im Nahen und Mittleren Osten, dem Souveränitätsstreit zwischen Russland und der Ukraine um die Krim oder Chinas Abenteuerlust und Expansionsstreben in angrenzenden Meeren. In manchen Fällen – etwa in Syrien – eskalieren

---

[4] Walter Russell Mead, The Return of Geopolitics: The Revenge of the Revisionist Powers. In: *Foreign Affairs* 93, Mai/Juni 2014.

lokale Grenzstreitigkeiten rasch zu Konflikten mit globalen Folgen durch Migration, Radikalisierung und zunehmenden Extremismus. Betrachtet man diese verschiedenen Bedrohungen in Kombination mit dem oben erwähnten Problem – den blockierten internationalen Institutionen –, dann erscheinen Verhandlungslösungen immer schwerer erreichbar.

Lösungen konzipieren

Die oben skizzierten Probleme stellen existierende Theorien grundlegend auf die Probe – sei es der neoliberale Institutionalismus, der Wohlstand und Frieden für die Welt durch den Aufbau von Institutionen verhieß, sei es der Konstruktivismus, der uns versprach, dass aus verstärkter Zusammenarbeit mit hoher Wahrscheinlichkeit Sozialisation erwachse. Was könnte angesichts dieser Herausforderungen getan werden? Hier folgend gebe ich drei Empfehlungen.

Empfehlung 1: Sich mit den „Anderen" auseinandersetzen – weil sie wichtig sind[5]

Einer der Gründe dafür, dass die Globalisierung unter Druck geraten ist, dass immer wieder multilaterale Blockaden auftreten und dass Länder sich von liberalen, institutionalistischen Lösungen abkehren und einen geopolitischen Kurs einschlagen,

---

[5] Amrita Narlikar, „Weil sie wichtig sind": Vielfalt anerkennen, Forschung globalisieren. GIGA *Focus Global 1*, April 2016, https://www.giga-hamburg.de/de/publikation/weil-sie-wichtig-sind, abgerufen am 15. Januar 2017.

liegt darin, dass mit diversen Akteuren viel zu wenig über den Zweck der internationalen Zusammenarbeit, wie sie für die Ära nach dem Zweiten Weltkrieg prägend war, beraten wurde. Es muss grundsätzlich neu darüber nachgedacht werden, welche globalen öffentlichen Güter auf der Prioritätenliste verschiedener Akteure ganz oben stehen und wofür sie auch bereit sind, die Kosten mitzutragen.

Dies bedeutet eine Auseinandersetzung mit Entwicklungsländern, die in der Zeit der Neuordnung 1945 nicht die Macht hatten, die Agenda mitzubestimmen, sowie mit ausgegrenzten Gruppen innerhalb der Industrie- und der Entwicklungsländer. Mehr noch: Diese Auseinandersetzung muss real sein und Substanz haben und darf nicht nur auf eine symbolische Political Correctness hinauslaufen; es wird nicht reichen, Alibi-Vertretern armer Länder einen Platz in Verhandlungsforen oder bei wissenschaftlichen Konferenzen zuzugestehen. Selbst diejenigen Länder des globalen Südens, die in verschiedenen internationalen Foren vertreten sind, werden bislang von uns im Westen oft nur durch unsere eigene Brille betrachtet, und wir erwarten von ihnen, dass sie unsere eigenen Verhaltensmuster kopieren. Tatsächlich ist ein weitaus besseres Verständnis der Weltanschauungen, Ambitionen und Ziele verschiedener Weltregionen und Bevölkerungen vonnöten – ob sie nun in wichtigen Gremien wie der G20 direkt vertreten sind oder durch Koalitionen mit anderen Entwicklungsländern indirekt ihre Stimme erheben.

Ausschlaggebend für diese Auseinandersetzung ist eine

enge Zusammenarbeit zwischen Wissenschaft und Praxis. Spitzenforschung über die Hoffnungen, Erwartungen und Herausforderungen von Regionen außerhalb der EU und der Vereinigten Staaten sowie über ihre philosophischen Traditionen und ihre Geschichtsverläufe ist unabdingbar, um diesen Prozess in Gang zu setzen. Dies ist in der Tat genau die Art der Forschung, die wir am GIGA entwickeln, und warum wir unterstreichen, wie wichtig es ist, uns einen „globalen Forschungsansatz" zu eigen zu machen. Wir hoffen, dass einige unserer Forschungsergebnisse westlichen Wissenschaftlerinnen und Wissenschaftlern sowie Regierungen helfen, den globalen Süden in seinen eigenen Zusammenhängen zu verstehen. Auf diese Weise, so glauben wir, können wir als Mittler zwischen EU/USA und der großen Mehrheit der Länder dienen, die mittlerweile viel mehr Bedeutung gewonnen haben, als weiterhin anerkannt wird.[6]

Verständnis, und das ist wichtig, bedeutet nicht, den Forderungen von Verhandlungspartnern einfach nachzugeben. Verständnis ist vielmehr wichtig, weil es hilft, rote Linien zu erkennen und zu kommunizieren. Wenn dieser Prozess mit der richtigen Einstellung angegangen wird, dann kann er entscheidend dazu beitragen, Fehleinschätzungen und Missverständnisse einzudämmen, und möglicherweise das kreative Ausloten neuer Verhandlungsspielräume innerhalb beiderseits anerkannter Grenzen erleichtern.

---

[6] Genaueres zu dieser Forschungsagenda findet sich in Narlikar 2016.

Empfehlung 2: Kompensation für Globalisierungsverlierer

Insgesamt sorgt die Globalisierung zwar für Gewinne, doch bringt sie für bestimmte Gruppen innerhalb der Länder auch Verluste. An dieser Stelle ist innerstaatliche Führungskompetenz von entscheidender Bedeutung. Auch wenn die Gesellschaftsverträge in verschiedenen Ländern je nach politischer Kultur erhebliche Unterschiede aufweisen, müssen Regierungen Mittel und Wege finden, die Liberalisierungsgewinne in der eigenen Bevölkerung zu verteilen. Die Wirtschaftskultur unterscheidet sich von Land zu Land und beruht sehr stark auf ganz konkreten Normen. Daher müssen Programme zur besseren Verteilung von Gewinnen und Verlusten jeweils im eigenen Land entwickelt werden.

Dabei ist anzumerken, dass internationale Organisationen mittels Forschung, Beratung, Hilfe und Handelspolitik auch die Suche nach kollektiven Lösungen unterstützen können. Letzten Endes haben Global-Governance-Institutionen jedoch nur begrenzte Kontrolle über die Maßnahmen ihrer Mitgliedstaaten zur besseren Verteilung der Globalisierungsgewinne. Die staatliche Politik sollte daher unbedingt der Versuchung widerstehen, internationale Handelsabkommen zum Sündenbock zu machen und die Grenzen für qualifizierte Migrantinnen und Migranten zu schließen. Dadurch kann sich das existierende Problem beträchtlich verschlimmern, wenn Gegenschläge anderer Ökonomien ausgelöst werden und besonders hohe Kosten für die ärmsten Verbraucher in dem Land entstehen, das protektionistische Maßnahmen umsetzt.

Vor allem dann, wenn die Welt sich weiter aufsplittert, könnte internationalen Organisationen eine größere Rolle zukommen. Sie könnten beispielsweise die Gesellschaftsverträge ihrer Mitgliedstaaten durch internationale Gesellschaftsverträge mit gerechteren Bedingungen der Mitsprache, des Austauschs und der Lastenverteilung ergänzen. Um dies zu gewährleisten, wären Personen, die internationale Verhandlungen führen, gut beraten, sich mit ihren diversen Gegenübern ernsthafter über die Frage der globalen öffentlichen Güter auseinanderzusetzen, wie unter Empfehlung 1 ausgeführt.

Empfehlung 3: Die Erfolge der Globalisierung wirksamer kommunizieren

In Wissenschaft und Praxis sind die Vorteile der Globalisierung den meisten so klar, dass die Argumente keiner Wiederholung bedürfen. Doch diese Selbstgefälligkeit hat einen hohen Preis, insbesondere angesichts der schlecht informierten, aber leidenschaftlichen Intensität der Globalisierungsgegnerinnen und -gegner. Am deutlichsten hat sich dies im Fall des Brexit-Referendums gezeigt, in dem die „Verbleib"-Kampagne wenig unternommen hat, um der Bevölkerung die Vorteile der EU-Mitgliedschaft zu erklären. Wenn die Globalisierung überleben soll, dann müssen die Argumente immer wieder durchdekliniert und für die allgemeine Öffentlichkeit übersetzt werden. Auch eine solche Initiative bedarf einer engen Zusammenarbeit zwischen Wissenschaft und Praxis und erfordert die Vertiefung bestehender und die Schaffung neuer Prozesse der Öffentlichkeitsarbeit. Selbst eine reformierte, aktualisierte und faire Globalisierungsvereinbarung wird ohne die Unterstützung der Bevölkerung wahrscheinlich keinen Bestand haben.

Schlussfolgerung

Um uns bei der Auseinandersetzung mit einigen dieser Fragen zu helfen und Wege zur möglichen Umsetzung innovativer und machbarer Lösungen aufzuzeigen, ist heute ein Denker und Lenker bei uns, der stets mit gutem Beispiel voranging – Minister Frank-Walter Steinmeier. Wir freuen uns sehr auf seine Analyse.

Übersetzung: Textpraxis, Marion Schweizer
Endfassung: GIGA, Julia Kramer

Federal Foreign Minister Frank-Walter Steinmeier

Breaches and Bridges — German Foreign Policy in Turbulent Times

Federal Minister for Foreign Affairs
Frank-Walter Steinmeier

Federal Foreign Minister Frank-Walter Steinmeier spoke upon invitation by the GIGA on 27 June 2016 at Hamburg City Hall.

Olaf,

Professor Narlikar,

Ladies and gentlemen,

I have just come from the beautiful Speicherstadt, which has been listed as a UNESCO World Cultural Heritage site. I would once again like to convey to you, Olaf, and all the people of Hamburg here today, my sincere congratulations on this achievement! However, the title of my speech – breaches and bridges – has nothing to do with the Speicherstadt ... The Speicherstadt is a brickbuilt reminder of why Hamburg is the gateway to the world for Germans. The history of the Hanseatic League, Hamburg's port and the famous civic spirit of Hamburg's citizens have a reputation that extends far beyond the city's boundaries.

A lesser-known fact, and wrongly so, is that here in Hamburg there is a concentration of academic expertise on central foreign and security policy issues that can be found hardly anywhere else in Germany. I am referring to the GIGA German Institute of Global and Area Studies, which celebrated its 50th anniversary two years ago. And I am also thinking of the Institute for Peace Research and Security Policy at the University of Hamburg, the Institute for Theology and Peace, the Carl Friedrich von Weizsäcker Centre for Science and Peace Research, the Max Planck Institute, the Körber Foundation, the Helmut Schmidt University and the Federal Armed Forces Command and Staff College – you get the idea. International expertise in Hamburg is considerable. Through research, teaching and advisory services, all these institutions help open doors to a world that seems increasingly complex and unpredictable.

"The world around us is changing more quickly than ever before. Those who want to understand it can't just sit back and accept the certainties from yesterday." Wise words – and they aren't mine, or even from Helmut Schmidt. They come from the GIGA and were written for its anniversary. Professor Narlikar, I was very happy to accept your invitation to speak here today on German foreign policy in turbulent and uncertain times. And thank you, Olaf, for allowing us to use this wonderful hall for this purpose.

***

We live in turbulent times. After the end of the Cold War, we thought that the triumphant progress of peace, freedom and democracy would begin throughout the world. Some even wrote books about "the end of history". Today, we are realising that that wasn't actually the case ... On the contrary, crises and conflicts are coming thick and fast, and liberal democracy seems to be on the wane in many places. That is no coincidence.

In 1989/1990, the old, cynical order of the Cold War collapsed – fortunately, in particular from our perspective as Germans. Yet since then, the world has failed to find a new order to replace it. Today, we are witnessing the wrestling for a new order, the power struggles between old and new powers, between state and nonstate players with a host of interests, ambitions, ideologies. Much of what has become familiar to us over the past years and decades is breaking up – and so far, we have not managed to put a stop to this process:

- Through its annexation of Crimea and the destabilisation of eastern Ukraine, Russia broke with the postwar order in Europe with which my generation grew up.

- Syria, Iraq, Libya – not only are the conflicts moving closer to Europe, they have arrived in our midst – in the form of refugees and many thousands of people seeking protection from the trouble spots in the Middle East.

- And there is more: the European Union is now also in the grip of crisis. On Thursday, we had to witness something that hardly anyone had considered possible, or wanted to consider possible – I, too, hoped right up until the end that the outcome would be different. The United Kingdom, a major and decisive partner, will leave the European Union. The forces trying to pull Europe apart are huge.

- And in the Brexit referendum – alongside its consequences for European policy – we must also recognise another dimension: the more complex the situation is, the louder the populist voices become. Whether we're talking about Trump or right-wing populists here in Europe, these are people who respond to the problems of an increasingly complex world with ready-made, simplistic, black and white slogans claiming that "Cutting ourselves off is the best solution. Leave the world and its problems outside!" And as much as responsible policymakers know how wrong these answers are, we have to embrace the sad fact that these populists exert a strong pull on voters in our democracies too.

What we are witnessing, at the end of the day, is a contradictory and confusing world. A world that on the one hand is growing ever more intertwined, but whose contrasts are colliding, unchecked, with ever more speed on the other. We are witnessing a world in search of a new order, and I suspect this search will continue for a long time yet.

***

If this is the case, it must have consequences for our foreign policy activities. Germany, as a country which maintains close economic, political and social ties with the global community – some studies even describe it as the most highly connected country in the world – is particularly reliant on a functioning, peaceful and rules-based international order. And since that is the case, we have to do all the more to preserve and develop this order.

The phrase, "Order must prevail" is often attributed to the Germans.

In itself it is a pretty meaningless statement – at least in foreign policy. Order is not an end in itself. Anyone who calls for order must define what kind of order and what goals we are working for. In our case, the desired goals are peace – justice – innovation – partnership. Perhaps you have already noticed these key words on the banners in the foyer. I'll explain towards the end of my speech what that means in the context of the United Nations.

***

These key words reflect our values. Yet, at the same time those of us engaged in foreign policy need to recognise the values other players on the international stage are seeking in their concepts of order. Where are the regional, cultural and societal differences? What are the stories and narrative patterns, the dreams and traumas of societies, which define the political and social structures over and above the existing order?

After a long day at the last UN General Assembly, I was standing one evening with a foreign minister counterpart outside our delegations' hotel in Manhattan, and we watched a few members of my delegation who were just leaving the hotel, and my colleague said to me: "Frank-Walter, I like you Germans really. Football, cars, beer ... But there's one thing I don't understand and I've always wanted to ask you about it: You Germans won't cross the road when the red light is on, even if there's not a car in sight. I could never get my people to do that. And why should they?"

This might be a trivial little story, but the question behind it isn't trivial: from where do orders, regulations, institutions derive their legitimacy and acceptance? In view of the upheaval and the calling into question of orders in this world – I only need to mention the dispute surrounding the South China Sea – awareness and debate of these kinds of fundamental and deep-seated cultural differences will become increasingly important.

And whoever is willing to engage in this debate will soon realise that an order that seems good to us – and now I'm not just talking about pedestrian crossings – will often not be perceived as such by others.

Speaking in Berlin recently, Achille Mbembe, a renowned political scientist from Cameroon, put it like this: "Your order is our disorder."

An openness towards other perspectives, the willingness to understand and promote understanding is a crucial factor in foreign policy. This willingness to understand and promote understanding is, after all, one of the qualities that has given Germany an excellent reputation as a mediator in many conflicts.

Sometimes we are criticised for "understanding Russia", "understanding Iran" – whatever fits at the time. I then have to ask myself what foreign policy is coming to if the desire to understand is perceived as an insult. Understanding doesn't automatically mean agreeing with someone. But without understanding, we cannot promote understanding!

As I see it, this means that greater attention needs to be paid to regional studies, such as those conducted by the GIGA on Africa, Latin America, Asia and the Middle East, in science, research and practice. That is why we are in the process of launching the Centre for East European and International Studies in Berlin to expand and deepen knowledge of this important region.

Professor Narlikar, what you recently formulated as a tenet for the social sciences – a move away from western centricism to a true pluralism of methods and perspectives – applies in a similar way to foreign policy if our goal is to work towards reaching truly shared concepts of order.

***

Anyway, enough social sciences – what does that mean specifically for German foreign policy? It almost makes me think of that old joke: Two social scientists get together. One of them has developed a political theory and outlines it. The other one listens, has a think and then says: "Hm, that sounds as if it works in practice – but does it work in theory?"

In practical foreign policy, work on tomorrow's order cannot be separated from today's acute conflict resolution. For it is in conflict resolution and crisis prevention that we can put what we like to call "effective multilateralism" into practice and prove its worth. Look at the range of partners:

- whether in the E3 plus 3 context on Iran,

- the Normandy format with France on Ukraine,

- in our current role as Chair of the OSCE, the Organization for Security and Cooperation in Europe,

- or in the International Contact Group on Syria, that brutal conflict that has been going on for far too long. I don't need to explain to you how crucial it is to have Iran and Saudi Arabia around the negotiating table as proxy powers wrestling for hegemony.

- And last but not least, consider the many facets of our engagement in the United Nations system: not only as one of the largest donors, but also as a contributor to the United Nations peace missions. I have just been to Mali with my French colleague, where we are currently engaged in arduous work to stabilise the country and implement the inter-Malian peace agreement under the auspices of the MINUSMA peace mission together with the Netherlands,

Switzerland, Belgium, Denmark, Estonia and the Czech Republic.

***

Effective multilateralism is thus proving its worth in very concrete terms in current crises. Yet, crisis management is not intended to be the focus of my address today, and believe me: I'm quite happy to take a break from all the conflicts ... I would like to look further afield: to the long-term challenges in a changing global order. I don't primarily wish to talk about NATO or Russia. Rather, the upcoming powers in Asia, Latin America, Africa and the Arab world, which are also the focus of the GIGA's research, are moving into our field of view.

Perhaps it is appropriate that today we are sitting in this wonderful hall, which automatically draws our gaze outwards into the wider world. Just take a look at the walls, where you can see the impressive paintings of Hugo Vogel – depicting Hamburg's proud history from Christianisation to industrialisation. But there is one constant that runs through all the pictures: the blue thread of the Elbe river. This river draws our eyes away from the square outside the City Hall overseas to the emerging economies.

For it is they, first and foremost China,

- who are increasingly calling into question regional balances of power and established rules – in the tensions surrounding the South China Sea, this issue is becoming ominously clear, an issue in which the validity of international law and its institutions are painfully put to the test,

- players who challenge international organisations and decision-making mechanisms,

- who demand reforms,

- and who establish new organisations based on their own concepts of order.

Germany is perceived as an "honest broker" in foreign policy, and we are therefore a desirable partner for these players, not only with regard to business and culture, but also in the creation of new elements of the global order.

I see this wherever I travel. Whether in China, India, Brazil or recently, in Mexico and Argentina. If, from time to time, it seems as if we are in a global competition where one country's gain is another's loss, that is too simplistic. There are many areas in which we can find joint solutions to conflicts and cooperate on building new structural elements.

Here are a few examples:

- Digital technology: In 2014, together with Brazil, we tabled a resolution in the United Nations on Internet privacy – an important basis for the ongoing search for order in this largely unregulated space.

- Migration: Together with Morocco we will assume the

Chairmanship of the Global Forum on Migration and Development next year. Here, the focus will be on exchange between countries of origin, transit and destination. We intend to discuss how migration can be organised fairly in a way that benefits all stakeholders. For one thing is clear: this topic is going to become even more relevant. Development of sustainable solutions is therefore also the focus of the Berlin Dialogue, which I have launched with heads of international organisations.

• Climate protection: Driving forces behind the adoption of the climate protection agreement last year were the numerous small island states, which are literally in deep water in the face of rising sea levels. Germany is a key partner for them, for we play a pioneering role in climate diplomacy. This also applies to states that are rather more problematic in this area, such as China, India and the Gulf States, and for whom we are a popular discussion partner with regard to the shift to green energy and renewables.

***

However, it is also clear – and here we share the view of many partners from the South – that we will only be able to successfully tackle these questions and other major issues if the United Nations' institutions do indeed reflect the world of the 21st century and not that of 1945. For this reason, we are working with Brazil,

India and Japan to bring about progress leading to a reform of the UN Security Council. And so we're back to the legitimacy of an order: the global acceptance and future viability of the United Nations depends on how representative the international community considers its institutions to be.

***

You will have noticed that I am speaking at length about the significance and role of the United Nations as a global regulatory framework. That is no coincidence. Tomorrow, a decision will be made in New York on which of our European partners will obtain a seat as non-permanent members of the UN Security Council for the next two years. Italy, the Netherlands and Sweden are standing for the two seats available.

I would like to take this as an opportunity to announce officially that Germany, too, will be campaigning again for a seat in this organ. To be precise, as a non-permanent member for 2019/2020. That means that in two years, we too, will stand for election by the UN General Assembly in New York. That still seems a good way off. But our campaign starts today and will get into full swing this autumn. So now, you know what the posh banners in the foyer are about.

Peace – justice – innovation – partnership, they read. Those are the key words of our campaign for a seat on the Security Council.

We firmly believe that we need the United Nations and the Security Council more than ever in our efforts to promote *peace* in these troubled times.

And although the UN Security Council has increasingly been on the receiving end of criticism and is, unfortunately, blocked on occasions, it nonetheless remains the only body capable of adopting conflict prevention and peacekeeping measures that are binding in international law. Despite all skepticism, in the last year, the Council has unanimously adopted 60 out of 63 resolutions. The Security Council is the central global crisis manager! In Africa particularly, UN peace missions are fostering stability, promoting reconciliation and protecting civilians. They are also doing an irreplaceable job in Israel and Lebanon. And the Security Council is the central forum for maintaining dialogue between the West and Russia and ensuring they retain their capacity to act, for example, in the struggle to find a solution for Syria.

Yet, even the Security Council is no longer merely concerned with traditional foreign and security policy. The Security Council now also debates the subjects of climate change, health, human rights, the rule of law and access to education – for they too are, at the end of the day, prerequisites for peace and security throughout the world. We want the Security Council to focus on the entire conflict cycle in its crisis management, from prevention and mediation to stabilisation and post-conflict peacebuilding. This philosophy of pursuing a forward-looking foreign policy is also behind the changes in German foreign policy in recent years.

Some of you have followed the steps we have taken to establish a Directorate-General for Crisis Prevention and Stabilisation at the Federal Foreign Office. Germany is contributing more civilian personnel, police officers and military forces to peace missions. And we are in the process of expanding the Center for International Peace Operations (ZIF) to make it a fully-fledged sending organisation.

***

The next step in our approach is: long-term peace is not possible without *justice*. Last year, with the 2030 Agenda for Sustainable Development, the international community adopted what could be described as a global company agreement. It is intended to prepare what Willy Brandt called for as early as 1979 in the visionary report of the so-called North-South Commission: an order for peace and justice. For in a globalised world, there can be no justice without peace, and no sustainable peace without justice.

- That is why we support the goals of the 2030 Agenda.

- That is why we work to promote the rule of law. Justice comes before power. The International Tribunal for the Law of the Sea, which is situated here in Hamburg, also, of course, pursues this goal.

- And that is why international promotion of human rights

is a key pillar of our foreign policy. And an integral part of our engagement in the United Nations! The violation of human rights is often an early warning of imminent conflict. For this reason, we are striving to foster closer cooperation between the Security Council in New York and the Human Rights Council in Geneva.

And if I can come back to Brandt, if peace and security on the one hand and sustainability, justice and distribution of resources on the other are globally interconnected, then I think we should focus our attention on the issue of justice and sustainability also in the context of our Chairmanship of the G20 in the coming year. That leads me to the third key word in our campaign: *innovation*. The highly-developed G20 states in particular need to address the question of how we can use technological progress, digitisation, the quantum leap in renewable energies and environmental technologies that we have made through Germany's shift to green energy – how we can use all that to drive economic and political ownership much further forward throughout the world, also in the Global South. This is in our own interests in creating a more stable and secure world, but it is also a question of justice.

***

Finally, ladies and gentlemen, the fourth key word of our candidacy spans all these other aspects: *partnership*.

Willy Brandt said: "We want to be a people of good

neighbours." At that time, when he assumed office as Federal Chancellor, this statement applied primarily to our European neighbours – France, Poland, and all those who had experienced terrible suffering at the hands of Nazi Germany. Today, when men, women and children from Aleppo, Damascus and Erbil are seeking refuge with us and when the United Nations 2030 Agenda for Sustainable Development has formulated the goal of a "global partnership" between 190 member states, we can still say: "We Germans want to be a people of good neighbours", but we ought now to add: "to those both near and far." In this spirit, I am campaigning for Germany's candidacy for a seat on the Security Council for the 2019/2020 period and would be delighted if you were all to back us in this endeavour.

Brüche und Brücken: Deutsche Außenpolitik in bewegten Zeiten

Bundesaußenminister
Frank-Walter Steinmeier

Außenminister Frank-Walter Steinmeier sprach auf Einladung des GIGA am 27. Juni 2016 im Hamburger Rathaus.

Lieber Olaf,

sehr geehrte Frau Professorin Narlikar,

sehr geehrte Damen und Herren,

ich komme gerade aus der schönen Speicherstadt, die von der UNESCO zum Weltkulturerbe erklärt wurde. Dazu möchte ich Dir, lieber Olaf, und allen Hamburgerinnen und Hamburgern unter Ihnen noch einmal ganz herzlich gratulieren! Der Titel meiner Rede – Brüche und Brücken – hat allerdings nichts mit der Speicherstadt zu tun …Die Speicherstadt ist in Ziegel gegossene Erinnerung, warum den Deutschen Hamburg das Tor zur Welt ist. Die Geschichte der Hanse, der Hamburger Hafen und der berühmte Hamburger Bürgersinn sind weit über die Grenzen der Stadt bekannt.

Zu Unrecht weniger bekannt ist, dass sich hier in Hamburg

wissenschaftlicher Sachverstand zu zentralen außen- und sicherheitspolitischen Themen konzentriert, wie wohl kaum anderswo in Deutschland. Damit meine ich das Leibniz-Institut für Globale und Regionale Studien, das GIGA, das vor zwei Jahren sein 50-jähriges Bestehen gefeiert hat. Und ich denke auch an das Institut für Friedensforschung und Sicherheitspolitik an der Universität Hamburg, das Institut für Theologie und Frieden, das Zentrum für Naturwissenschaft und Forschung, das Max-Planck-Institut, die Körber-Stiftung, die Helmut-Schmidt-Universität und die Führungsakademie der Bundeswehr – you get the idea: Der internationale Sachverstand in Hamburg ist groß. Alle diese Institutionen tragen dazu bei, durch Forschung, Lehre und Beratung Tore zu einer Welt zu öffnen, die zunehmend komplex und unvorhersehbar scheint.

„Die Welt um uns herum verändert sich, schneller als jemals zuvor. Wer sie verstehen will, darf sich nicht ausruhen auf den Gewissheiten von gestern". Weise Worte – sie stammen nicht von mir, auch nicht von Helmut Schmidt, sondern vom GIGA, damals zum Jubiläum geschrieben. Ihre Einladung, Frau Professorin Narlikar, hier und heute über die deutsche Außenpolitik in bewegten und ungewissen Zeiten zu sprechen, habe ich sehr gerne angenommen. Und danke, Olaf, dass Du uns diesen schönen Festsaal dafür zur Verfügung stellst.

***

Wir leben in bewegten Zeiten. Nach dem Ende des Kalten Krieges dachten wir, dass Frieden, Freiheit und Demokratie nun ihren weltweiten Siegeszug antreten würden. Manche schrieben Bücher über das „Ende der Geschichte". Heute stellen wir fest: Ganz so war es dann doch nicht ... Im Gegenteil: Die Krisen und Konflikte überschlagen sich geradezu, und die liberale Demokratie scheint vielerorts auf dem Rückzug. Das ist kein Zufall.

1989/1990 ist die alte, zynische Ordnung des Kalten Krieges untergegangen – zum Glück, gerade für uns Deutsche. Doch seither hat die Welt noch keine neue Ordnung gefunden. Heute entlädt sich das Ringen um neue Ordnung, das Kräftemessen zwischen alten und neuen Mächten, zwischen staatlichen und nicht-staatlichen Akteuren, mit einer Vielzahl von Interessen, Ambitionen, Ideologien. Vieles von dem, was uns über die vergangenen Jahre und Jahrzehnte vertraut geworden ist, das geht gerade zu Bruch – und wir haben es bislang nicht geschafft, diesen Prozess zum Halten zu bringen:

- Mit der Annexion der Krim und der Destabilisierung der Ostukraine hat Russland mit der Nachkriegsordnung in Europa gebrochen, mit der meine Generation aufgewachsen ist.

- Syrien, Irak, Libyen – die Konflikte rücken nicht nur näher an Europa heran, sondern sie sind mitten unter uns angekommen – in der Gestalt von Flüchtlingen und Abertausenden Schutzsuchenden aus den Krisenherden des Mittleren Ostens.

- Und noch eine Steigerung kommt hinzu: der Krisenmodus hat die Europäische Union selbst erfasst. Am Donnerstag mussten wir erleben, was kaum jemand für möglich hielt oder halten wollte – auch ich habe bis zuletzt gehofft, dass es anders kommen würde. Großbritannien, ein großer und entscheidender Partner, wird die Europäische Union verlassen. Die Fliehkräfte, die an Europa zerren, sind enorm.

- Und man muss in der Brexit-Abstimmung – neben ihren europapolitischen Folgen – auch noch eine weitere Dimension erkennen: je komplexer die Lage, desto lauter die Lockrufe der Populisten. Ob Trump, oder ob Rechtspopulisten auch bei uns in Europa: das sind Leute, die auf die Probleme einer immer komplexeren Welt die ganz einfachen, die ganz schwarz-weißen Parolen bereithalten nach dem Motto: „Abschottung ist die beste Lösung! Lasst die Welt mit ihren Problemen draußen!" Und so sehr verantwortliche Politik weiß, wie falsch diese Antworten sind, so sehr müssen wir uns damit auseinandersetzen, dass solche Populisten leider auf Wählerinnen und Wähler auch in unseren Demokratien eine starke Sogwirkung entfalten.

Was wir sehen, unterm Strich, ist eine widersprüchliche und unübersichtliche Welt. Eine Welt, die einerseits immer enger zusammenwächst, aber deren Gegensätze zugleich immer schneller und ungebremst aufeinanderprallen. Wir sehen eine

Welt auf der Suche nach neuer Ordnung, und ich vermute, diese Suche wird noch lange anhalten.

***

Wenn dem so ist, dann muss das Folgen haben für unser außenpolitisches Handeln. Deutschland, als wirtschaftlich und politisch und gesellschaftlich eng mit der Welt vernetztes Land – manche Studien sagen sogar: als meistvernetztes Land der Welt – ist ganz besonders auf eine funktionierende, friedfertige und regelbasierte internationale Ordnung angewiesen. Und weil das so ist, müssen wir umso mehr tun für den Erhalt und die Weiterentwicklung dieser Ordnung.

Den Deutschen wird gern der Satz zugeschrieben: „Ordnung muss sein".

Für sich betrachtet ist das eine ziemlich sinnlose Aussage – zumindest in der Außenpolitik. Ordnung ist ja kein Selbstzweck. Wer nach Ordnung ruft, muss dazusagen: Für welche Ordnung und welche Ziele von Ordnung setzen wir uns ein? Für uns heißen die Zielvorstellungen: Frieden – Gerechtigkeit – Innovation – Partnerschaft. Vielleicht haben Sie die Schlagworte schon auf den Bannern im Eingangsbereich gesehen. Was es damit im Kontext der Vereinten Nationen auf sich hat, will ich gegen Ende meiner Rede erläutern.

***

In diesen Schlagworten spiegelt sich *unsere* Werthaltung. Aber gleichzeitig müssen wir uns in der Außenpolitik bewusst darüber sein, wonach *andere Akteure* auf der Weltbühne in ihren Ordnungsvorstellungen suchen. Wo liegen regionale, kulturelle, gesellschaftliche Unterschiede? Was sind die Geschichten und Erzählmuster, die Träume und Traumata von Gesellschaften, die die politischen und sozialen Verhältnisse über die faktische Ordnung hinaus begründen?

Nach einem langen Tag während der letzten UNO-Generalversammlung stand ich abends mit dem Außenminister eines befreundeten Landes vor unserem Delegationshotel in Manhattan und wir schauten einem Teil meiner Delegation hinterher, der da gerade das Hotel verließ, und da sagte der Kollege zu mir: „Frank-Walter, eigentlich mag ich Euch Deutsche: Fußball, Autos, Bier … Aber eins verstehe ich nicht und wollte ich Dich immer schon fragen: Ihr Deutschen geht bei Rot nicht über die Straße, auch wenn weit und breit kein Auto kommt. Das könnte ich meinen Leuten nie beibringen – wieso auch?"

Das mag eine triviale kleine Anekdote sein, aber die Frage dahinter ist nicht trivial: Woher beziehen Ordnungen, Regeln, Institutionen eigentlich ihre Legitimität und Akzeptanz? Angesichts der Verwerfungen und Infragestellung von Ordnungen auf dieser Welt – ich nenne hier nur den Streit um das Südchinesische Meer – wird das *Wissen* und die *Auseinandersetzung* über solche zugrunde liegenden, kulturellen, tief verwurzelten Unterschiede umso wichtiger.

Und wer sich auf diese Auseinandersetzung wirklich einlässt, dem wird schnell klar, dass eine Ordnung, die *uns* gut erscheint – und ich spreche jetzt nicht nur von Fußgängerampeln – oftmals von anderen nicht so gesehen wird.

Ein renommierter Politikwissenschaftler aus Kamerun, Achille Mbembe, hat es neulich in Berlin so formuliert: „Eure Ordnung ist unsere Unordnung."

Die Offenheit für andere Sichtweisen, die Bereitschaft zum Verstehen und zur Verständigung ist Voraussetzung von Außenpolitik. Es ist nicht zuletzt die Bereitschaft zu Verstehen und Verständigung, die Deutschland einen exzellenten Ruf als Vermittler in vielen Konflikten verschafft hat.

Manchmal werden wir dafür kritisiert – wahlweise als „Russland-Versteher" oder als „Iran-Versteher" usw. Ich frage mich dann immer: Wo kommt Außenpolitik eigentlich hin, wenn Verstehen-Wollen zum Schimpfwort wird? Verstehen heißt ja nicht automatisch Einverstanden-Sein. Aber ohne Verstehen kann es keine Verständigung geben!

Für mich heißt das, dass die Regionalstudien, wie sie das GIGA zu Afrika, Lateinamerika, Asien und Nah- und Mittelost betreibt, in Wissenschaft, Forschung und Praxis wieder an Stellenwert gewinnen müssen. Daher setzen wir gerade auch das Zentrum für Osteuropa- und internationale Studien in Berlin aufs Gleis, um das Wissen über diese wichtige Region zu erweitern und zu vertiefen.

Frau Professorin Narlikar, was Sie kürzlich als These für

die Sozialwissenschaften formuliert haben – weg vom West-Zentrismus hin zu einem echten Pluralismus von Methoden und Sichtweisen –, das gilt in ähnlicher Weise für die Außenpolitik, wenn wir das Ziel haben, zu wirklich gemeinsamen Vorstellungen von Ordnung zu gelangen.

***

So, genug Sozialwissenschaft – was heißt das für die deutsche Außenpolitik konkret? Ich muss sonst fast an den alten Witz denken: Treffen sich zwei Sozialwissenschaftler. Der eine hat eine politische These entwickelt und trägt sie vor. Der andere hört zu, denkt kurz nach und sagt: „Hm, das klingt, als funktioniert es in der Praxis – *aber funktioniert es auch in der Theorie?*"

In der praktischen Außenpolitik ist die Arbeit an der Ordnung von morgen nicht trennbar von der akuten Konfliktlösung im Heute. Denn in der Konfliktlösung und auch in der Krisenprävention beweist sich und übt sich das, was wir gern den „effektiven Multilateralismus" nennen. Schauen Sie auf die Reihe der Partner:

- ob im Rahmen der E3 plus 3 zu Iran,

- dem Normandie-Format mit Frankreich zur Ukraine,

- aktuell im Vorsitz der OSZE, der Organisation für Sicherheit und Zusammenarbeit in Europa,

- oder der internationalen Kontaktgruppe zu Syrien, diesem schon viel zu lange währenden, grausamen Konflikt. Ich brauche Ihnen nicht zu erklären, wie essenziell es ist, Iran und Saudi-Arabien als Stellvertretermächte, die um Hegemonie ringen, mit am Verhandlungstisch zu haben.

- Und schauen Sie nicht zuletzt auf unsere vielfältigen Einsätze im System der Vereinten Nationen: nicht nur als einer der größten Financiers, sondern auch als Beitragende zu den Friedensmissionen der Vereinten Nationen. Zusammen mit meinem französischen Kollegen war ich gerade in Mali, wo wir unter dem Dach der Friedensmission MINUSMA gemeinsam mit den Niederlanden, der Schweiz, Belgien, Dänemark, Estland und Tschechien an dem mühsamen Weg arbeiten, Mali zu stabilisieren und das innermalische Friedensabkommen umzusetzen.

***

Effektiver Multilateralismus beweist sich also in den akuten Krisen ganz konkret. Aber Krisenmanagement soll nicht der Fokus meines heutigen Vortrages sein, und glauben Sie mir: Mir ist eine Pause von den Krisen mal ganz recht … Ich möchte den Blick darüber hinaus wenden: auf die langfristigen Herausforderungen in einer sich wandelnden Weltordnung. Ich möchte dabei auch nicht in erster Linie über die NATO oder Russland sprechen. Sondern in unser Blickfeld rücken zunehmend die aufstrebenden Mächte in Asien, Lateinamerika, Afrika und der arabischen Welt, denen sich auch die Forschung des GIGA widmet.

Vielleicht ist es da ganz passend, dass wir hier heute in diesem wunderbaren Saal sitzen, der unseren Blick ja ganz automatisch in die weite Welt hinaus führt. Schauen Sie sich mal um an den Wänden: da sehen Sie die prächtigen Wandgemälde von Hugo Vogel – sie zeigen die stolze Geschichte Hamburgs von der Christianisierung bis zur Industrialisierung. Aber eine Konstante zieht sich durch alle Bilder: das blaue Band der Elbe. Dieser Fluss zieht unseren Blick hier vom Rathausplatz nach Übersee, hin zu den aufstrebenden Ländern.

Denn sie sind es, China zuvorderst,

- die zunehmend regionale Machtgleichgewichte und vereinbarte Regeln in Frage stellen – in den Spannungen um das Südchinesische Meer wird diese Frage schon bedrohlich deutlich, eine Frage, in der die Geltung des Völkerrechts und seiner Institutionen empfindlich auf die Probe gestellt sein wird,
- Player, die internationale Organisationen und Entscheidungsmechanismen herausfordern,
- die Reformen verlangen,
- und die neue Organisationen auf Basis eigener Ordnungs- vorstellungen gründen.

Deutschland gilt in der Außenpolitik als „ehrlicher Makler", und deshalb sind wir für diese Player ein gesuchter Partner, nicht nur was Wirtschaft und Kultur angeht, sondern auch bei der Gestaltung von neuen Elementen der globalen Ordnung.

Das wird mir deutlich, wo immer ich hinreise. Ob nach

China, Indien, Brasilien oder zuletzt nach Mexiko und Argentinien. Wenn zuweilen der Eindruck entsteht, wir befänden uns in einem globalen Wettstreit, in dem des Einen Gewinn des Anderen Verlust ist, dann greift das zu kurz. Es bestehen viele Anknüpfungspunkte für gemeinsame Lösungen in Konflikten, und für die gemeinsame Arbeit an neuen Ordnungselementen.

Ein paar Beispiele:

- Thema Digitalisierung: Gemeinsam mit Brasilien haben wir 2014 in den Vereinten Nationen eine Initiative zur Privatheit im Internet gestartet – eine wichtige Grundlage für die weitere Suche nach Ordnung in diesem noch weitgehend ordnungsfreien Raum.

- Thema Migration: Gemeinsam mit Marokko übernehmen wir im kommenden Jahr den Vorsitz im „Global Forum on Migration and Development". Im Mittelpunkt steht hier der Austausch zwischen Herkunfts-, Transit- und Zielländern. Wir wollen diskutieren, wie Migration für alle Beteiligten gewinnbringend und fair gestaltet werden kann. Denn eines ist klar: Dieses Thema wird an Bedeutung noch gewinnen. Die Entwicklung nachhaltiger Lösungsansätze steht deswegen auch im Mittelpunkt des Berliner Dialogs, den ich mit den Leitern internationaler Organisationen begonnen habe.

- Thema Klimaschutz: Treibende Kräfte für den Abschluss des Klima-Vertrags im letzten Jahr waren auch die zahlreichen kleinen Inselstaaten, denen angesichts steigender Meeresspiegel das sprichwörtliche Wasser bis zum Hals steht. Für sie ist Deutschland ein wichtiger Partner, denn wir haben eine Vorreiterrolle bei der Klimaaußenpolitik. Das gilt übrigens auch für die in dieser Thematik eher schwierigeren Staaten wie China, Indien oder die Golfstaaten, für die wir in puncto Energiewende und erneuerbare Energien ein gesuchter Gesprächspartner sind.

***

Fest steht aber auch – und hier teilen wir die Sichtweise vieler Partner aus dem Süden –, dass wir diese und andere große Themen nur werden meistern können, wenn die Institutionen der Vereinten Nationen tatsächlich die Welt des 21. Jahrhunderts widerspiegeln – und nicht die von 1945. Deshalb setzen wir uns mit Brasilien, Indien und Japan für Fortschritte ein hin zu einer Reform des UNO-Sicherheitsrats. Da sind wir wieder bei Legitimität von Ordnung: Die globale Akzeptanz und Zukunftsfähigkeit der Vereinten Nationen hängt davon ab, wie repräsentativ ihre Institutionen in den Augen der Staatengemeinschaft sind.

***

Sie haben gemerkt: Ich rede ausführlich über die Bedeutung

und Rolle der Vereinten Nationen als globaler Ordnungsrahmen. Das ist kein Zufall. Morgen wird in New York darüber entschieden, welche unserer europäischen Partner für die kommenden zwei Jahre als nichtständige Mitglieder im UNO-Sicherheitsratsrat sitzen werden. Italien, die Niederlande und Schweden kandidieren für die zwei Sitze, die zur Wahl stehen.

Ich will das zum Anlass nehmen, um heute offiziell bekannt zu geben, dass sich auch Deutschland erneut für einen Sitz in diesem Gremium bewirbt. Genau gesagt als nichtständiges Mitglied für die Jahre 2019/20. Das bedeutet, dass in zwei Jahren auch wir uns in New York zur Wahl durch die UNO-Generalversammlung stellen werden. Das scheint noch eine Weile hin zu sein. Aber unsere Kampagne beginnt heute und wird in diesem Herbst zu Hochtouren auflaufen. Jetzt wissen Sie also, was die schicken Aufsteller im Foyer zu bedeuten haben …

Frieden – Gerechtigkeit – Innovation – Partnerschaft, steht darauf. So haben wir unsere Kampagne für einen Sitz im Sicherheitsrat überschrieben.

Für uns ist klar: Wir brauchen die Vereinten Nationen und den Sicherheitsrat mehr denn je im Bemühen um *Frieden* in dieser unfriedlichen Zeit.

Und auch wenn der UNO-Sicherheitsrat zunehmend in die Kritik gekommen ist und in der Tat leider manchmal blockiert ist, so bleibt er doch das einzige Organ, das völkerrechtlich bindende Maßnahmen zur Konfliktprävention und Friedenssicherung beschließen kann. Bei aller Skepsis: Im letzten Jahr hat der Rat 60 von 63 Resolutionen im Konsens verabschiedet. Der Sicherheitsrat ist zentraler globaler Krisenmanager! Gerade in Afrika leisten UNO-Friedensmissionen Stabilisierung, fördern Versöhnung und schützen Zivilisten. Auch in Israel und Libanon bleiben sie unersetzlich. Und der Sicherheitsrat ist das zentrale Forum, um den Westen und Russland im Dialog und handlungsfähig zu halten, zum Beispiel im Ringen um eine Lösung für Syrien.

Aber: Auch im Sicherheitsrat geht es nicht mehr nur um klassische Außen- und Sicherheitspolitik. Mit den Themen Klima, Gesundheit, Menschenrechte, Rechtsstaatlichkeit, Zugang zu Bildung setzt sich der Sicherheitsrat inzwischen auseinander – denn auch sie sind am Ende Voraussetzung für Frieden und Sicherheit weltweit. Wir wollen, dass der Sicherheitsrat im Krisenmanagement den gesamten Konfliktzyklus in den Blick nehmen sollte: von Prävention, Mediation bis hin zu Stabilisierung und Konfliktnachsorge. Diese Philosophie einer vorausschauenden Außenpolitik steht ja auch hinter den Neuerungen der deutschen Außenpolitik in den letzten Jahren. Einige von Ihnen haben begleitet, wie wir eine Abteilung für Krisenprävention und Stabilisierung im Auswärtigen Amt eingerichtet haben. Deutschland beteiligt sich verstärkt an Friedensmissionen mit zivilem Personal, Polizei und Militär. Und wir sind dabei, das Zentrum für Internationale Friedenseinsätze zu einer vollwertigen Entsendeorganisation aufzubauen.

***

Der nächste Schritt in unserem Ansatz heißt: Nachhaltiger Frieden nicht ohne *Gerechtigkeit*. Mit der 2030 Agenda für Nachhaltige Entwicklung hat die Staatengemeinschaft im vergangenen Jahr so etwas wie einen globalen Gesellschaftsvertrag geschlossen. Er soll vorbereiten, was Willy Brandt schon 1979 in dem visionären Bericht der sogenannten „Nord-Süd-Kommission" gefordert hat: eine Ordnung für Frieden und Gerechtigkeit. Denn in einer globalisierten Welt gibt es Gerechtigkeit nicht ohne Frieden, und nachhaltigen Frieden nicht ohne Gerechtigkeit.

- Deshalb unterstützen wir die Ziele der Agenda 2030.

- Deswegen setzen wir uns für die Förderung von Rechtsstaatlichkeit ein. Recht geht vor Macht. Dazu dient natürlich auch der Internationale Seegerichtshof, der hier in Hamburg zuhause ist.

- Und deshalb ist der weltweite Einsatz für Menschenrechte ein Grundpfeiler unserer Außenpolitik. Und: ein integraler Bestandteil unseres Engagements in den Vereinten Nationen! Wenn Menschenrechte verletzt werden, ist das oftmals ein erstes Warnsignal für einen bevorstehenden Konflikt. Daher setzen wir uns dafür ein, dass der Sicherheitsrat in New York und der Menschenrechtsrat in Genf enger miteinander kooperieren.

Und wenn ich nochmal auf Brandt zurückkomme, wenn also Frieden und Sicherheit einerseits und Nachhaltigkeit, Gerechtigkeit und Verteilung andererseits global miteinander verbunden sind, dann, finde ich, sollten wir uns dem Thema Gerechtigkeit und Nachhaltigkeit auch im Rahmen unseres G20-Vorsitzes im kommenden Jahr widmen. Da bin ich beim dritten Stichwort unserer Kampagne: *Innovation.* Gerade die hochentwickelten Staaten der G20 müssen sich doch die Frage stellen, wie wir technologischen Fortschritt, Digitalisierung, den Quantensprung bei erneuerbaren Energien und Umwelttechnologien, den wir in der deutschen Energiewende gemacht haben – wie wir all das nutzen, um wirtschaftliche und politische Teilhabe viel stärker weltweit, auch im globalen Süden, voranzubringen. Das ist in unserem Eigeninteresse für eine stabilere, sicherere Welt, aber es ist auch eine Frage der Gerechtigkeit.

***

Zuletzt, meine Damen und Herren, steht über all diesen Aspekten das vierte Leitmotiv unserer Kandidatur: *Partnerschaft.*

Willy Brandt hat gesagt: „Wir wollen ein Volk guter Nachbarn sein". Damals, bei seinem Amtsantritt als Bundeskanzler, galt dieser Satz noch in erster Linie unseren europäischen Nachbarn – Frankreich, Polen und allen, die unter Nazi-Deutschland Schlimmstes erlitten hatten. Heute, da Männer, Frauen und Kinder aus Aleppo, Damaskus oder Erbil bei uns Zuflucht suchen, und auch die Agenda 2030 der Vereinten Nationen das Ziel einer „globalen Partnerschaft" unter 190 Mitgliedstaaten formuliert hat, gilt noch immer: „Wir Deutschen wollen ein Volk guter Nachbarn sein", doch wir sollten heute hinzufügen: „den nahen und den fernen Nachbarn gleichermaßen". In diesem Sinne werbe ich für einen deutschen Sitz im Sicherheitsrat 2019/20, und ich würde mich freuen, wenn Sie alle uns dabei unterstützen würden.

Federal President Dr Frank-Walter Steinmeier

Curriculum vitae

5 January 1956	Born in Detmold, Lippe District
1966 – 1974	Grammar school in Blomberg
1974 – 1976	Military service
1976 – 1982	Read law and from 1980 political science at the JustusLiebigUniversität in Giessen
1982	First state law examination
1983 – 1986	Legal training in Frankfurt am Main and Giessen
1986	Second state law examination
1986 – 1991	Academic assistant, Chair of Public Law and Political Science, Department of Law, Giessen University
1991	Desk officer for media law and policy, State Chancellery of Land Lower Saxony
1993 – 1994	Head of the Office of the Minister-President of Land Lower Saxony
1994 – 1996	Head of the State Chancellery Department responsible for policy guidelines and interministerial coordination and planning
1996 – 1998	State Secretary and Head of the State Chancellery of Land Lower Saxony
1998 – 1999	State Secretary in the Federal Chancellery and Commissioner for the Federal Intelligence Services
1999 – 2005	Head of the Federal Chancellery
November 2005 – October 2009	Federal Minister for Foreign Affairs
November 2007 – October 2009	Deputy Chancellor
2009 – 2013	Chair of the SPD Parliamentary Group
December 2013 – January 2017	Federal Minister for Foreign Affairs
Since 19 March 2017	Federal President of the Federal Republic of Germany

Bundespräsident Dr. Frank-Walter Steinmeier

Lebenslauf

5. Januar 1956	geboren in Detmold, Kreis Lippe
1966 – 1974	Besuch des Neusprachlichen Gymnasiums in Blomberg
1974 – 1976	Bundeswehr
1976 – 1982	Studium der Rechtswissenschaft, seit 1980 zusätzlich der Politikwissenschaft, an der Justus Liebig-Universität in Gießen
1982	Erste Juristische Staatsprüfung
1983 – 1986	Juristischer Vorbereitungsdienst in Frankfurt/M. und Gießen
1986	Zweite Juristische Staatsprüfung
1986 – 1991	Wissenschaftlicher Mitarbeiter am Lehrstuhl für öffentliches Recht und Wissenschaft von der Politik, Fachbereich Rechtswissenschaft, Universität Gießen
1991	Referent für Medienrecht und Medienpolitik in der Niedersächsischen Staatskanzlei
1993 – 1994	Leiter des persönlichen Büros des niedersächsischen Ministerpräsidenten
1994 – 1996	Leiter der Abteilung für Richtlinien der Politik, Ressortkoordinierung und -planung
1996 – 1998	Staatssekretär und Leiter der Niedersächsischen Staatskanzlei
1998 – 1999	Staatssekretär im Bundeskanzleramt und Beauftragter für die Nachrichtendienste
1999 – 2005	Chef des Bundeskanzleramts
November 2005 – Oktober 2009	Bundesminister des Auswärtigen
November 2007 – Oktober 2009	Vizekanzler
2009 – 2013	Vorsitzender der SPD-Bundestagsfraktion
Dezember 2013 – Januar 2017	Bundesminister des Auswärtigen
Seit 19. März 2017	Bundespräsident der Bundesrepublik Deutschland